Akhal-Teke "The Golden Horse of the desert" For Kids

Nature Books for Kids

By

K. Bennett

Mendon Cottage Books

JD-Biz Publishing

Read More Amazing Animal Books

Purchase at Amazon.com

Table of Contents

Introduction

*He knows when you're happy, He knows when you're comfortable, He knows when you're confident, And he always knows when you have carrots. ~**Author Unknown***

***

"The Golden Horse of the desert! Exceptional movement, agility, speed, stamina."

This is how ***Horsetalk.co.nz*** describes the Akhal-Teke. Do you think they're right? You may not know a lot about this horse, so let's try to find out what makes it so special.

Are you ready? Then let's get started!

The Akhal – Teke is an amazing horse with a beautiful coat that shines in the sun! That's why many call it 'the golden horse of the desert.' Can you guess why these horses are called "golden horses?" You're right! It is because of their beautiful coat. It shines in the light. Look at the pictures in this book and you will see it is true.

This lovely horse comes all the way from Turkmenistan. They are so loved in this country that this horse is the National Emblem. Do you know what that means? An emblem is a symbol of something else. It can represent a family, nation or organization. In this case, the Akhal Teke represents the nation of Turkmenistan.

Having a beautiful coat does not mean Akhal-Teke are not strong horses. They adapt very well to where they live and they are known as one of the oldest horse breeds. Would you like to know how tough they are?

In 1935, Turkmen riders went from a place called Ashgabat (Known as: Ashkabad) to Moscow. It took 84 days to make the trip and a 3 day crossing over 235 miles of desert. The most amazing part of this story is how they did this WITHOUT water! I am thirsty even thinking about it.

Do you think this would have been possible without the help of this magnificent horse? I don't think so!

The Akhal- Teke is a wonderful horse. It is so adaptable it can be used as a jumping horse, sport horse, racing, endurance riding horse and more.

You might think this means the horse is tough and not friendly. But this is not true. Many people say this horse is not only "golden" in its color, but also "golden" in its personality. Keep reading to find out why!

And Remember: Every single creature on this beautiful planet can teach us something wonderful. So take a few minutes to learn about these noble animals that have captured our imagination, our minds and definitely…our hearts!

Chapter 1

Taking a stroll in the field

History: The exact origins of the Akhal- Teke are hard to know, but many think it came from the tribes of Turkmenistan. If you are curious about where this country is located, ask your parent or a guardian to help you search. If you look at maps of the world you will find Turkmenistan located on the Asian continent. *Did you find it?*

The Ancestors of this beautiful horse is called the Nisean horse. The Akhal-Teke is also similar to another breed called Turkoman horse. Today, we find thousands of these horses around the world, but especially in Turkmenistan and Russia.

At the start of their known history, Akhal-Teke's were very valuable to the people of Turkmenistan. They used them for raiding because of their steady nature and endurance. The interesting part of this custom was the way they prepared the horse for the raids. Would you like to know how they did it?

Wikipedia.org explains what happened: *"The stallions were covered from head to tail with up to seven layers of felt, which kept their coat short and shiny. Before raids they were put on a sparse diet to prepare them for the long ride through the desert with no water and hardly any feed."*

A very hard training plan, don't you agree? But these horses did more than help their masters in the raids. Terri Fender from *Equitrekking* said these horses participated in 'surprise attacks, fast retreats, transport and racing!'

During the 19th century was a great time for the Akhal-Teke. Many used them to ride as war horses and they were sent to the Russian Czar as gifts. Do you know what a Czar is? A Czar is a leader or ruler.

During the 20th century, the Russians tried to improve the breed of this magnificent animal by crossing it with English thoroughbreds. The idea was to improve the size of the horse.

Sadly, as the years went by many of these horses were killed for their meat, especially during the war. This lowered the number of horses greatly and very few remained.

But that was the past and today we have good news! There are thousands of Akhal-Teke horses in the world. The largest group is found in Russia, and others are found around Europe and a little in the UK.

Little by little, this beautiful horse is returning to our lives. Would you like to get one?

FUN FACTS FOR KIDS: What is HANDS?

This is a neat way of measuring horses. The measurement refers to hands, literal hands!

Many years ago, people did not have rulers or measuring sticks like we have today. So they used whatever they had…and they had hands. So horses are measured in hands. You can do this too! One hand is 4 inches.

So if a horse is 15 hands multiply this by 4. (15 x 4) and you will get 60 inches. And if a horse is 16 hands multiply this number by 4. (16 x 4) and you will get 64 inches.

Now that you know how to do it, you can measure the other horses for yourself. Have fun!

Let's learn numbers!

Looking good!

A horse by any other name: Let's talk about the name of the Akhal – Teke. Are you curious to know where it comes from? To understand this, we have to return in history to the year 1881.

During that time, Turkmenistan became a part of the Russian Empire. A Russian general had seen the horses when he fought the people of the tribe and he admired them very much. So he decided that he wanted some of these horses for himself. What did he do?

He started a breeding farm. And he renamed the horses he saw after the Teke Turkmen tribe. Can you guess where they lived? Near an Oasis. Can you guess the name?

Well, think about it this way…We have the second part of the horse's name which is TEKE because they came from the Teke Turkmen tribe. And what is the first part of the horse's name? Yes! AKHAL.

This was the name of the Oasis: Akhal. So this Russian general renamed the horses ***Akhal-Teke***, and there you go!

These horses are very steady and do not scare easily. They do not just jump when something appears behind the bush, and this makes this horse a great ride!

Feels good to jump in the grass!

Characteristics: Akhal Teke stands at approximately 14.2 to 16 hands. Do you remember how to find the inches? Then calculate the hands for yourself and you will find the inches!

Weight: Usually they weigh between 900 – 1000 lbs.

These horses have a very distinct color. It is called "golden bucksin" or "palomino." This color variation is the result of a cream gene.

Do you remember what genes are? Genes are found inside the cell of all living things. This applies to horses too! These instructions tell us what the animal will look like, what color it will be, how tall, how friendly and more.

In the case of Akhal – Teke's, the cream gene gives the horse a beautiful coat in vibrant colors. There is also bay, chestnut, black and grey. They also have beautiful almond shaped eyes, but sometimes they can be "hooded."

They also have a beautiful head but not much mane and tail. And they are blessed with a long neck and long, thin ears and long, lean legs.

You might think of the word: Elegant when you think of this horse.

Out for a soft run

Training: These horses are highly intelligent. So intelligent, loyal and loving they are almost "dog-like" in their affections. So this will give you an idea of their personality.

Some horses are friendly to everyone but Akhal-Tekes are not like that. Terri Fender from *Equitrekking* says this breed "tend to want to bond to one person or family." Some call it a 'one-man' horse. So Akhal-Teke's do not bond to just anyone!

This means if someone other than the owner is riding the Akhal-Teke, they may have some problems with the horse. Remember: they are 'dog-like' in their affections. And a dog is usually faithful to their owner and family, but no one else. So the horse feels the same way!

And when it comes to training, the Akhal-Teke prefers certain types of skills. ***Dressage training*** is recommended. Would you like to know what this is?

Dressage training: Dressage training has existed for a very long time. The purpose of this training is to have your horse be the best it can be. The USDF (United States Dressage Federation) organization lists different levels for this type of skill. There are five levels:

-Training level
-First level
-Second level
-Third level
-Fourth level

Before you begin this type of training, there are several things to do. ***Wikihow.com*** suggests the following steps.

1- Both you and your horse need to know each other. And you need to know if you can trust each other. So a close relationship is very important before any training can begin!

2- You have to start to work on the way your horse walks or trots. This is referred to as a gait. It is very important for your horse to walk in the right way.

3- Transitions: This is when you want your horse to change from one movement to another. It is important that this step is done in a smooth manner. It should be just like putting one footstep in front of the other without tripping over your feet!

4- Your position in the saddle should look comfortable and balanced! And your heels should be down at all times.

5 – Practice makes perfect. To get good at any skill, you need to do it over and over again. Practicing with your horse is a great way to get good at riding him!

Of course there are many other steps to dressage that is very important. But these are some of the basic ideas. If you want to learn more, ask your parent or a guardian to help you research.

Chapter 2

Akhal-Teke's are truly magnificent creatures. But there is still more to learn about them. Because of their natural abilities, Akhal-Teke's are good at many different skills.

This includes: Dressage (which we talked about), eventing, racing and endurance riding. Would you like to know what each one of these things mean? (Source: *Wikipedia.org*)

Dressage: This word is actually French. This term is usually translated as "training." Another name for it is "Horse ballet." Have you seen a ballerina on stage? In a similar way, these horses are very good at doing certain movements in a graceful way. They usually do this with very little help from their riders.

It starts from a simple level and then gets more difficult as time goes on. The scores are from 0 to 10, and each one of these numbers point to something. *Wikipedia.org* labels the score like this:

0 – *Not performed*
1 – *Very bad*
2 – *Bad*
3 – *Fairly bad*
4 – *Insufficient*
5 – *Marginal*
6 – *Satisfactory*
7 – *Fairly good*
8 – *Good*
9 – *Very good*
10 – *Excellent*

Show jumping: This type of sport has very different terms like: Stadium jumping, open jumping or jumpers. The name tells you what it is: Jumping horses! These horses jump over many objects. Then they turn and change directions many times. However, horses must jump over the objects without touching them. They also have a specific time for each jump. Akhal – Teke's are very good at jumping. Do you remember their long, lean legs? They are very good at flying through the air gracefully!

Eventing: Another name for this sport is "Horse trials." Riders and their horses compete in different events. It includes 3 types of events in one. Cross country, dressage and show jumping. Another word for this is Triathlon. You probably know that triathlon means 3! So this is 3 competitions at one time. This competition can last for one, two or three days depending on the rules. But to be chosen to participate, both horse and rider need to pass a test at the beginning! Usually both horse and rider look their best to impress the judges.

Racing: You probably know this means more than one horse running against the other. Have you seen racing shows on TV? The winner is the horse that gets to the finish line. Or at least the horse that runs faster than the others! This type of sport is thousands of years old, but it still happens today.

Endurance Riding: This type of race really puts a horse to the test. This is long – distance riding. So a horse needs to have a lot of energy to ride for a long time. The winner of the race is the one that gets to the finish line. However, since this is a long race the horse has to stop from time to time so a Vet can check to make sure it can keep going. Most of the endurance races in the United States are between 50 to 100 miles long. There are also shorter rides for riders who don't have a lot of experience.

So much fun to run!

CURIOUS FACT FOR KIDS:

Akhal – Teke's are descendants of famous horses that the Chinese people loved very much. These horses are known as "blood – sweaters."

Do you think this name is funny? *PetMD.com* says 'the nomadic tribes had a strange way of caring for their horses. They used to let them "sweat" out their extra fat so they could stay lean." Isn't that interesting? Think of it like exercise. If you want to get rid of extra pounds, sweating is usually a great way to do it.

This type of behavior was very important for the horses. During times when the horses had little food to eat, being slim was not a bad thing!

Look at my shiny coat!

Diseases: Of course these horses get sick too. And there are different types of sickness that affect them. One of them is called naked foal syndrome. How does it happen? Well, when a horse is born it has no hair, mane or tail. Sometimes the teeth grow badly and the stomach can be sick too.

Because the skin has no protection, the horse may get very dry and scaly skin. And it can get very bad sunburns too, especially during the summer. And during the winter, it can get a lot of infections in the lungs. Poor little horse!

Sadly, this type of disease is not good. And many (If not all) times, the baby horse does not last that long and dies.

There is also another disease known as Wobbler syndrome. This causes the horse to walk funny. This is called a wobbly gait. This problem happens because of a problem with the neck / spinal area. This type of sickness gets worse over time and can affect the horse very much!

Happily, these diseases do not always affect the horse. And if you care for them very well, they will be healthy, happy and strong!

Feels good to stretch my legs!

Famous Akhal – Teke's: There are many famous Akhal-Teke horses. One well known horse is Absent. This was during the Olympics of 1960. Absent was a black stallion and he got the gold medal with a score of 82.4%. But that is not all he won. He won 6 more medals for his outstanding skills!

Chapter 3

There is no doubt Akhal-Teke's are unique horses! Here are a few additional facts about horses in general including Akhal- Teke's you may like to know. (Source: ***Onekind.org***)

-A horse can express its emotions in many different ways. It can use its face, eyes and ears to tell you how it feels!

-Horses are great at keeping watch. It is rare to see a herd with everyone snoozing at one time. There is usually one horse standing as a lookout, and his job is to warn the others if danger comes near!

- Avoid standing behind a horse. They have great vision, but there are a couple of blind spots. Can you guess what the back part of the horse is? Yes! It's a blind spot. If the horse gets angry or scared, guess what he may do if you stand directly behind him?

-Horses are great at listening! They can turn their ears in different ways to improve their hearing. If you whisper and say something bad about your horse, they just might hear you!

- Horses can help people get better when they have mental or health problems. This is called: *Equine Assisted Therapy*.

-Akhal Teke's are known for their loyal personality. They are also very sensitive in nature and they form a very strong bond to their owners. This makes Akhal-Teke's one of a kind!

-In Europe, there is a commercial that talks about the symbols of the country and why they are important. One of the symbols is the Akhal-Teke. This shows how valuable it is for the people!

-In the United States there are approximately 500 registered Akhal – Teke's. This is according to Terri Fender of *Equitrekking.com.*
-There is an Akhal-Teke organization of America. Their goal is to "preserve and promote" this magnificent horse.

-If you own an Akhal-Teke in Russia it is a sign that you have some money. It is just like having an expensive house or car.

Important symbol

GENERAL HORSE TIPS FOR KIDS:

If you are able to get a horse, you will need to care for it. So here are some tips you can think about: (Frank Bell- *Horsewhisperer.com*)

-Your horse's diet is very important. Some horses have very hot blood and some have cooler blood. If your horse has hot blood, they will need less protein in their diet.

-Learn how to properly discipline your horse. Remember: These animals are very sensitive and in the case of the Akhal-Teke's, they are very intelligent. Let them know when they are getting too out of control! This can be with a shhhhh noise or a firm tone to let them know who is in control.

-If the horse's head is high it means your horse is not relaxed. They may be uptight. If their head if low they are relaxed. Try to ensure your horse is always relaxed. This will help them feel good and both of you will enjoy the ride.

-Horses love to get your tender rubs and soft patting. Things like rubbing their ears, nose, eyes and mouth is great. And if you massage it, it's even better!

-If a horse is trained really well, he or she will invite YOU for a ride. You should be looking for the invitation! Then you know you will enjoy an awesome ride.

-Your horse can sense your moods and behavior. If you are confident your horse will be confident too!

-You should feed your horse from a bucket and not your hand. (This is the recommendation, but I feel it is better to feed them with your hand from time to time! It seems to generate more trust and respect, but that is just my humble opinion on the subject. What do you think?)

Conclusion

So much fun to ride!

In conclusion: Horses are beautiful creatures, and Akhal –Teke's are no exception. The "golden horse of the desert" is a magnificent horse breed and there are many things we can still learn about them! Just like any other creature, they have feelings, emotions and need to be treated with love, kindness and respect.

They are strong, faithful, loyal and willing to work hard. They are also ready to go the "extra" mile if you want them to. Why don't you take the time to learn a little bit more about them? You will be amazed at what you find. If you don't know where to look, ask your teacher, a parent or guardian to help you. Choose something you really like about this horse and learn a bit more about it.

I hope this book has taught you just how wonderful it is to learn about these magnificent animals. Akhal-Teke's like all other creatures are truly one of nature's magnificent wonders!

Author Bio

K. Bennett loves to write for both children and adults. Many different subjects are interesting to develop, but writing for children is special to her heart.

Her favorite pastimes include reading, traveling and discovering new things. Each of these activities helps to fuel her imagination and acts like a blank canvas waiting for more stories.

She is intrigued with fantasy elements like hidden worlds and faraway lands. Basically anything that gets her imagination soaring to new heights!

Her writing credits include children books online, short stories for online magazines, and two novellas listed at Amazon.com

Our books are available at

1. Amazon.com

2. Barnes and Noble

3. Itunes

4. Kobo

5. Smashwords

6. Google Play Books

This book is published by

JD-Biz Corp

P O Box 374

Mendon, Utah 84325

http://www.jd-biz.com/

Read more books from John Davidson

Amazon.com Author Link